WHAT'S YOUR COLOR?
COLORING BOOK FOR ADULTS

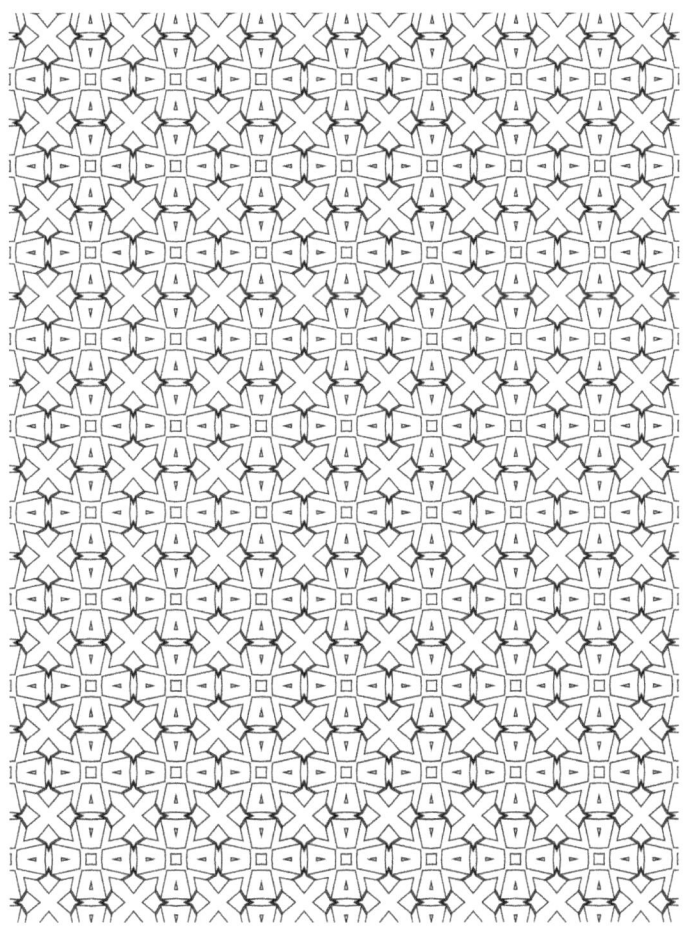

Grownups Stress Manual With
Over 40 Symmetrical Geometric Patterns

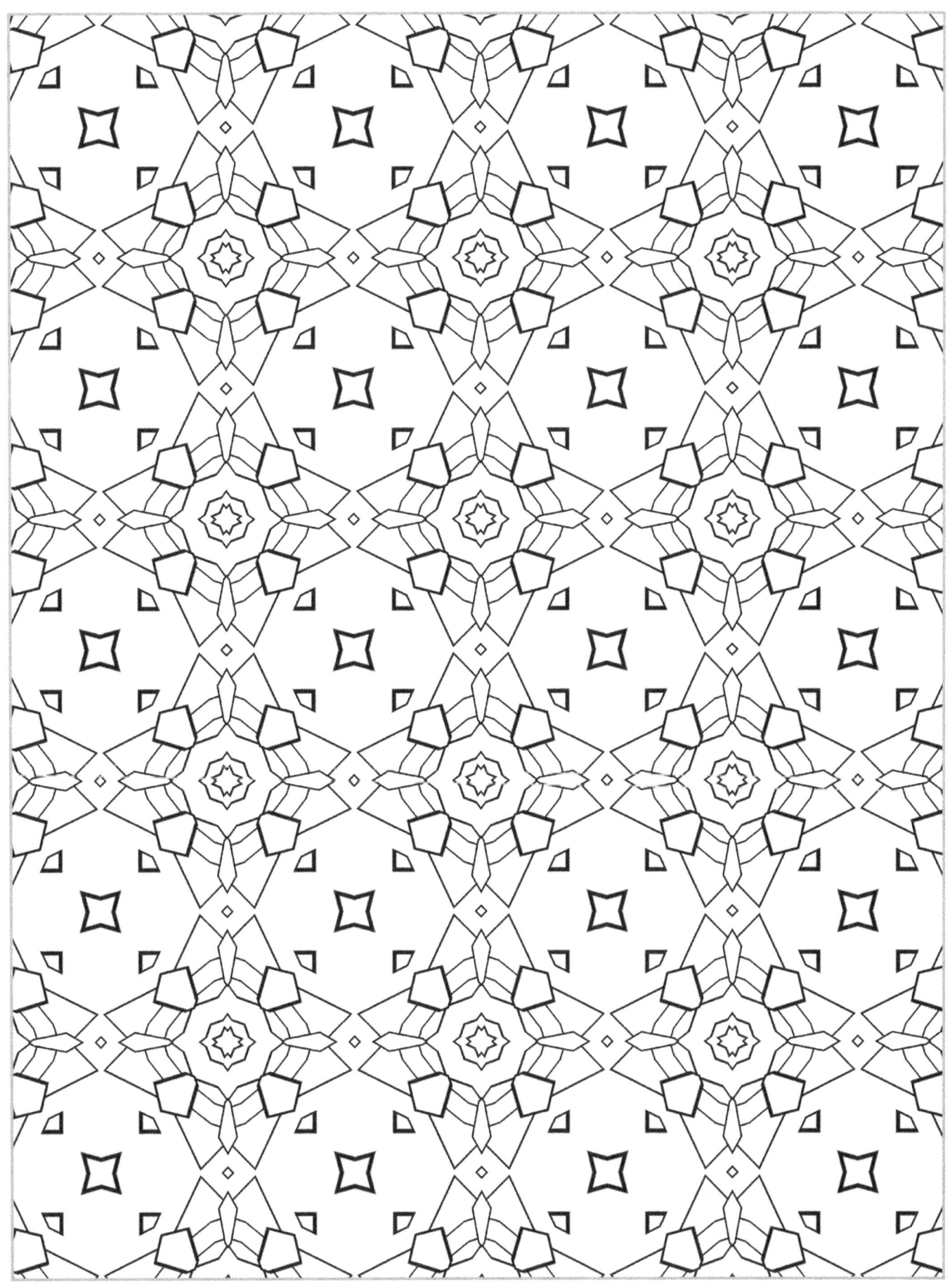

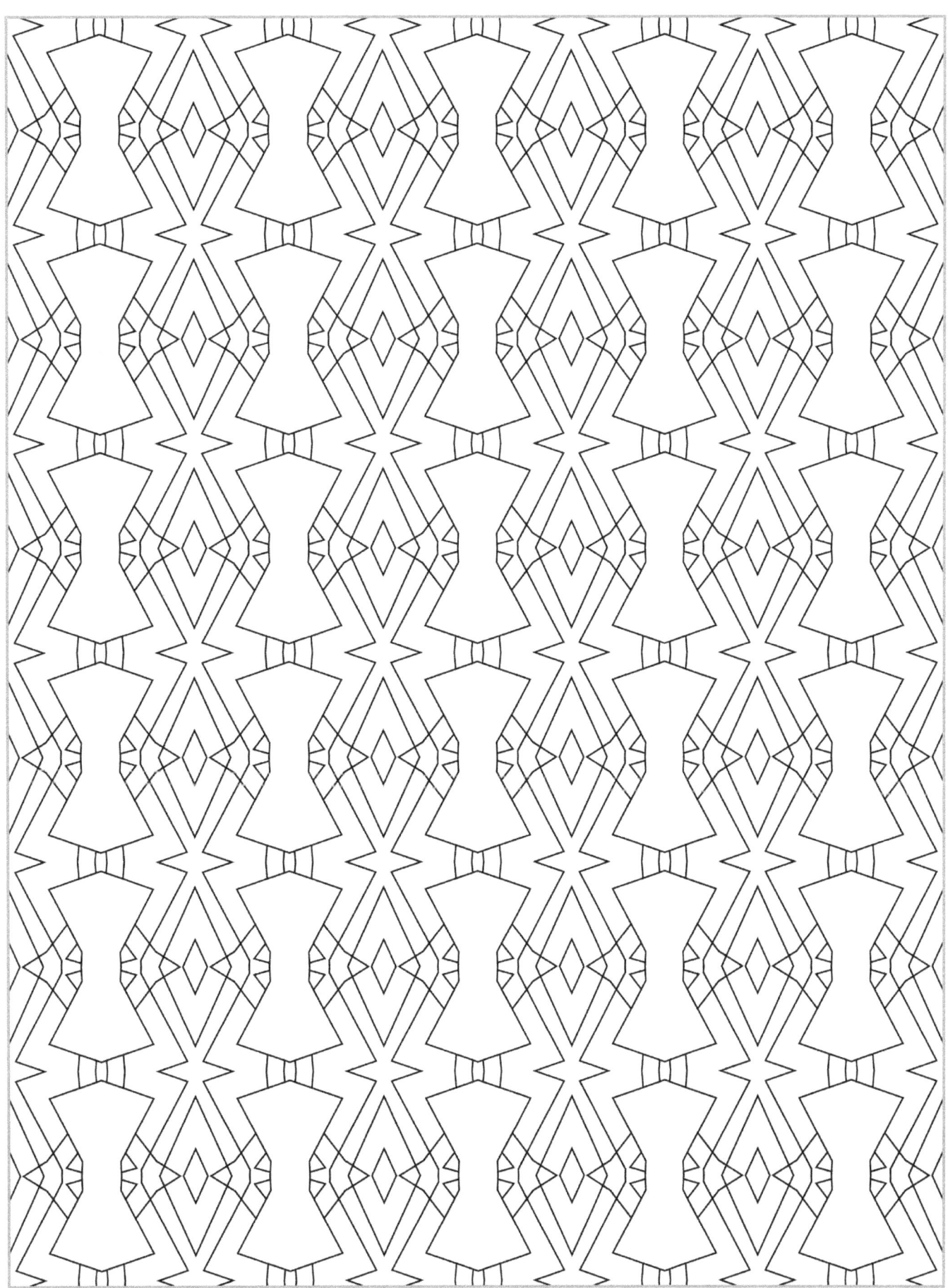

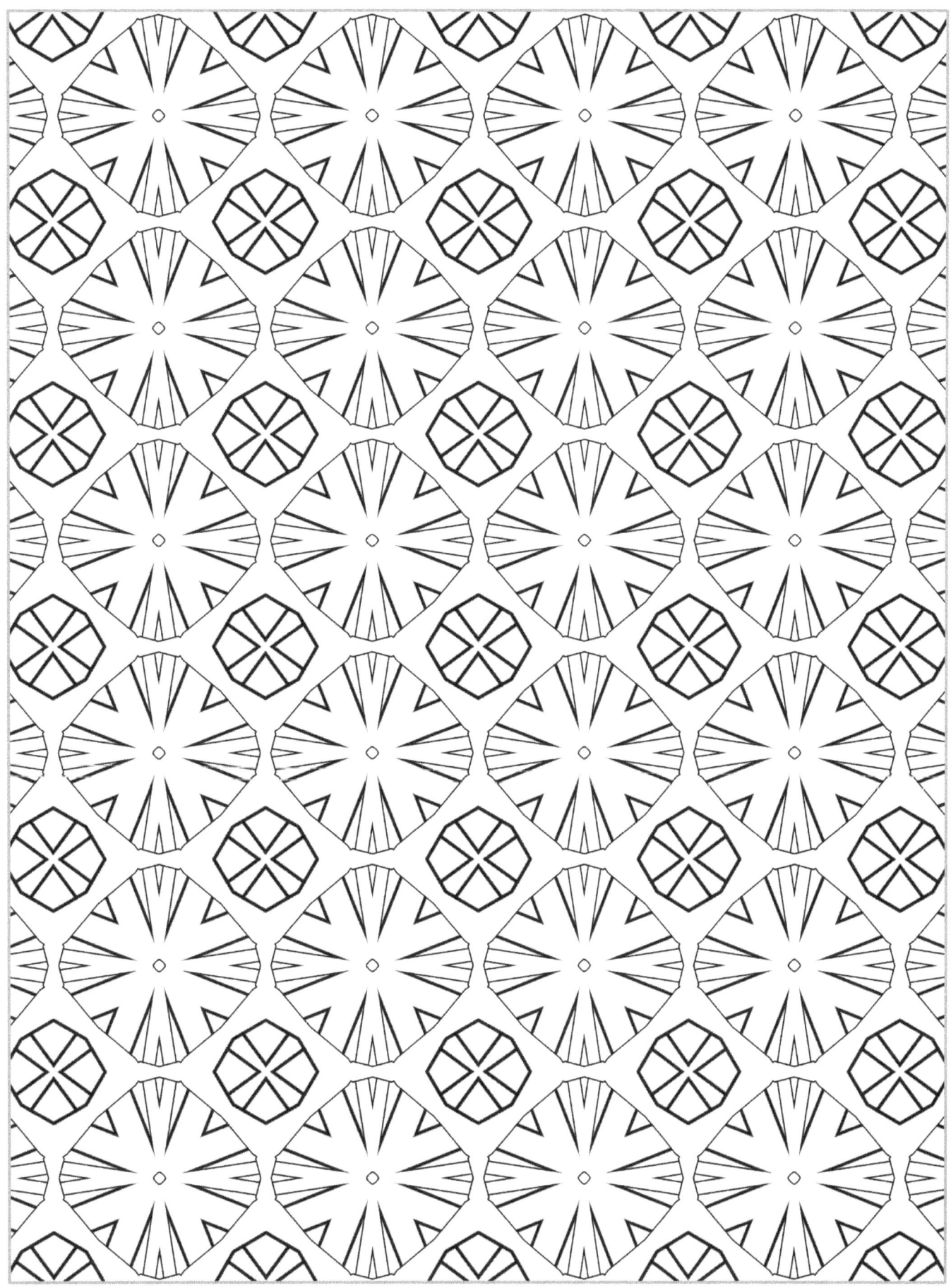

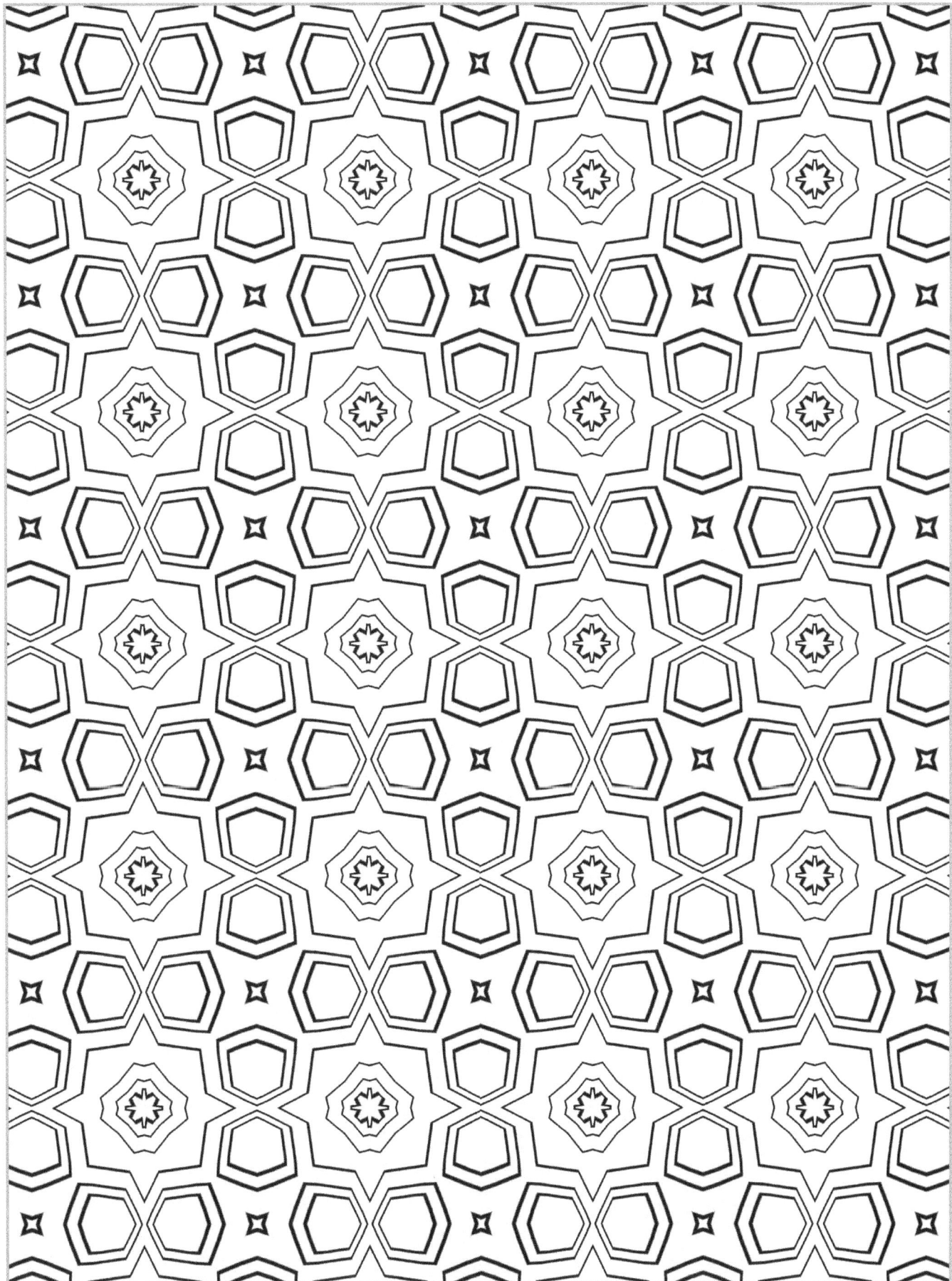

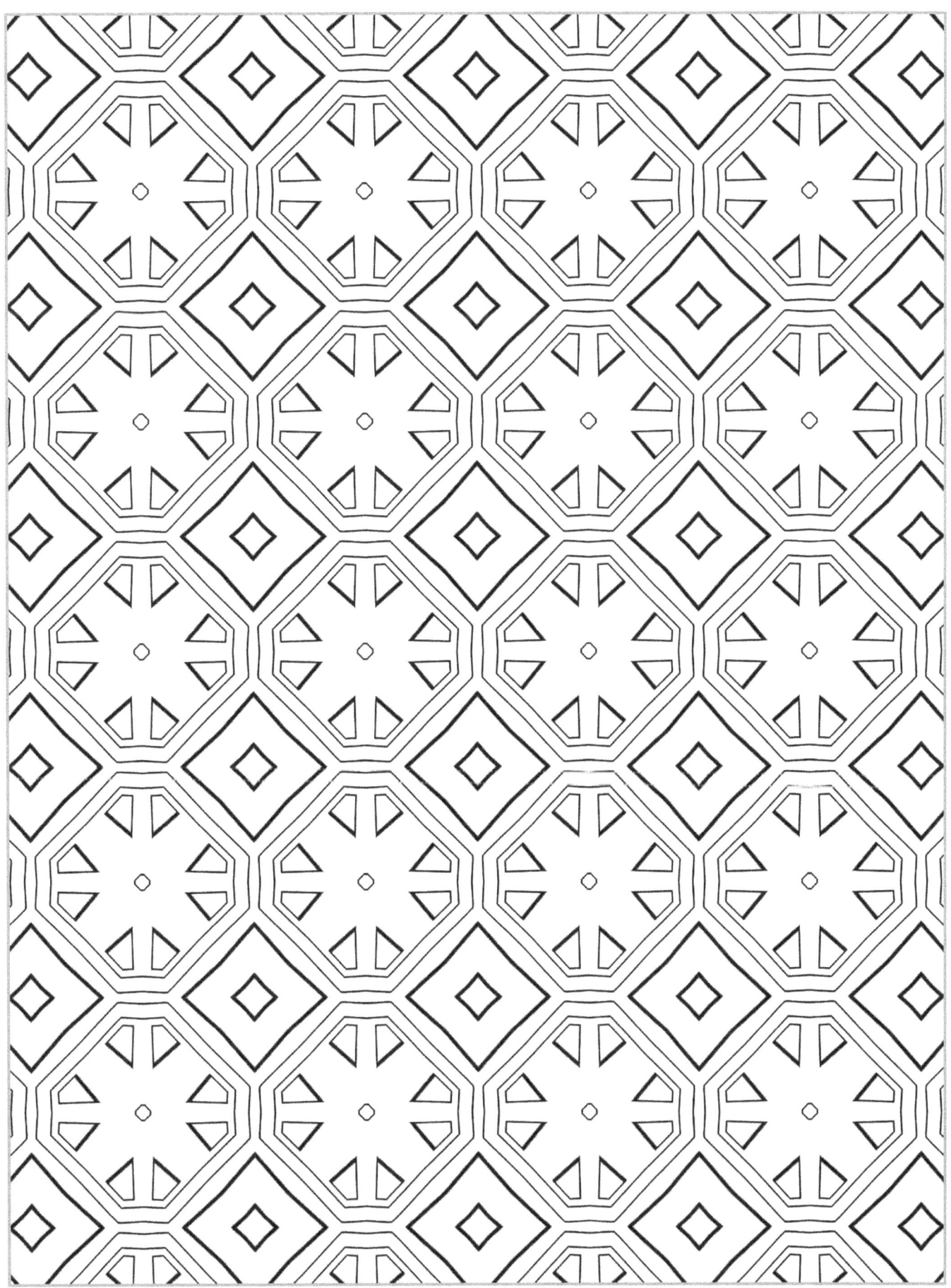

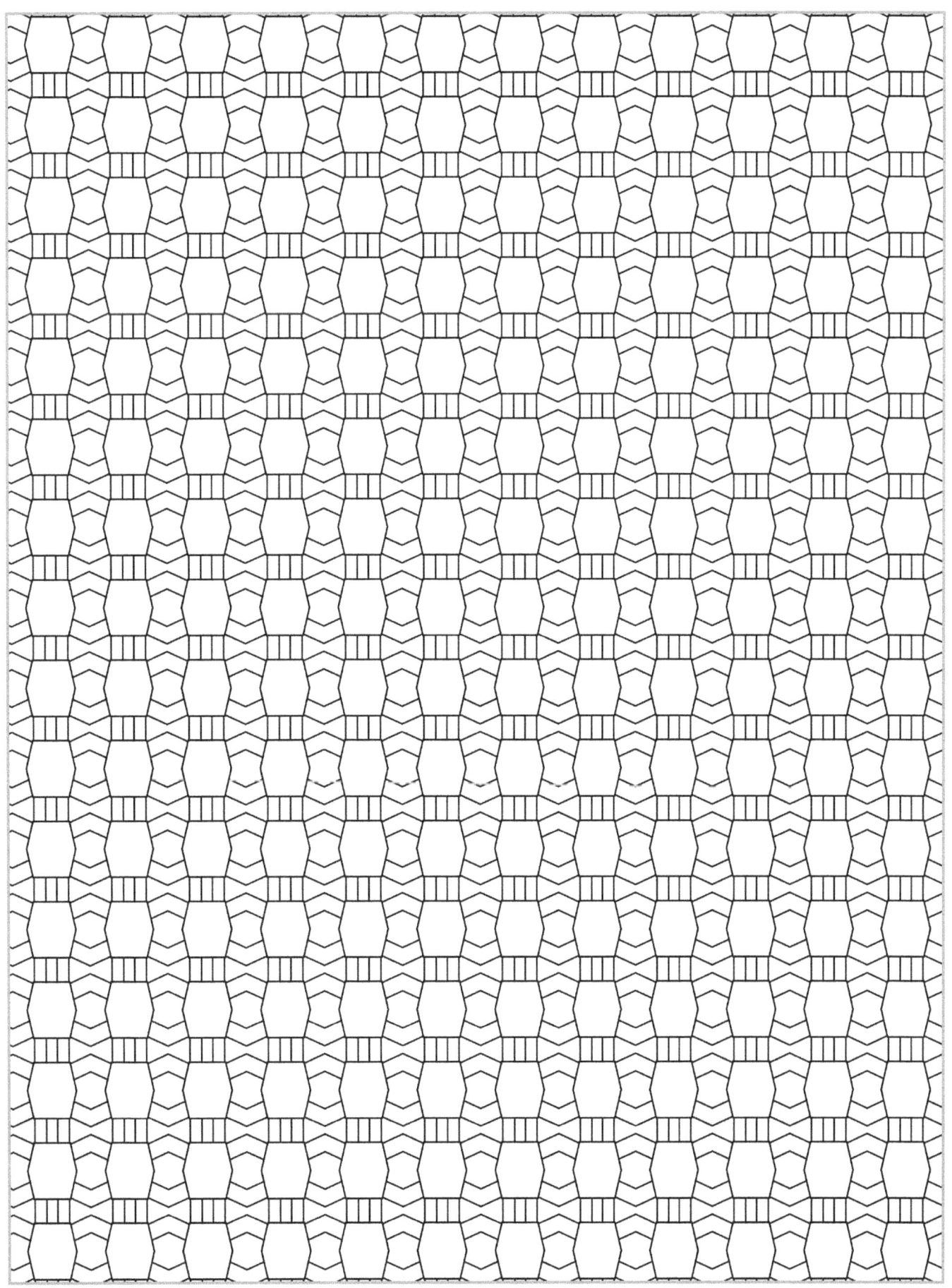

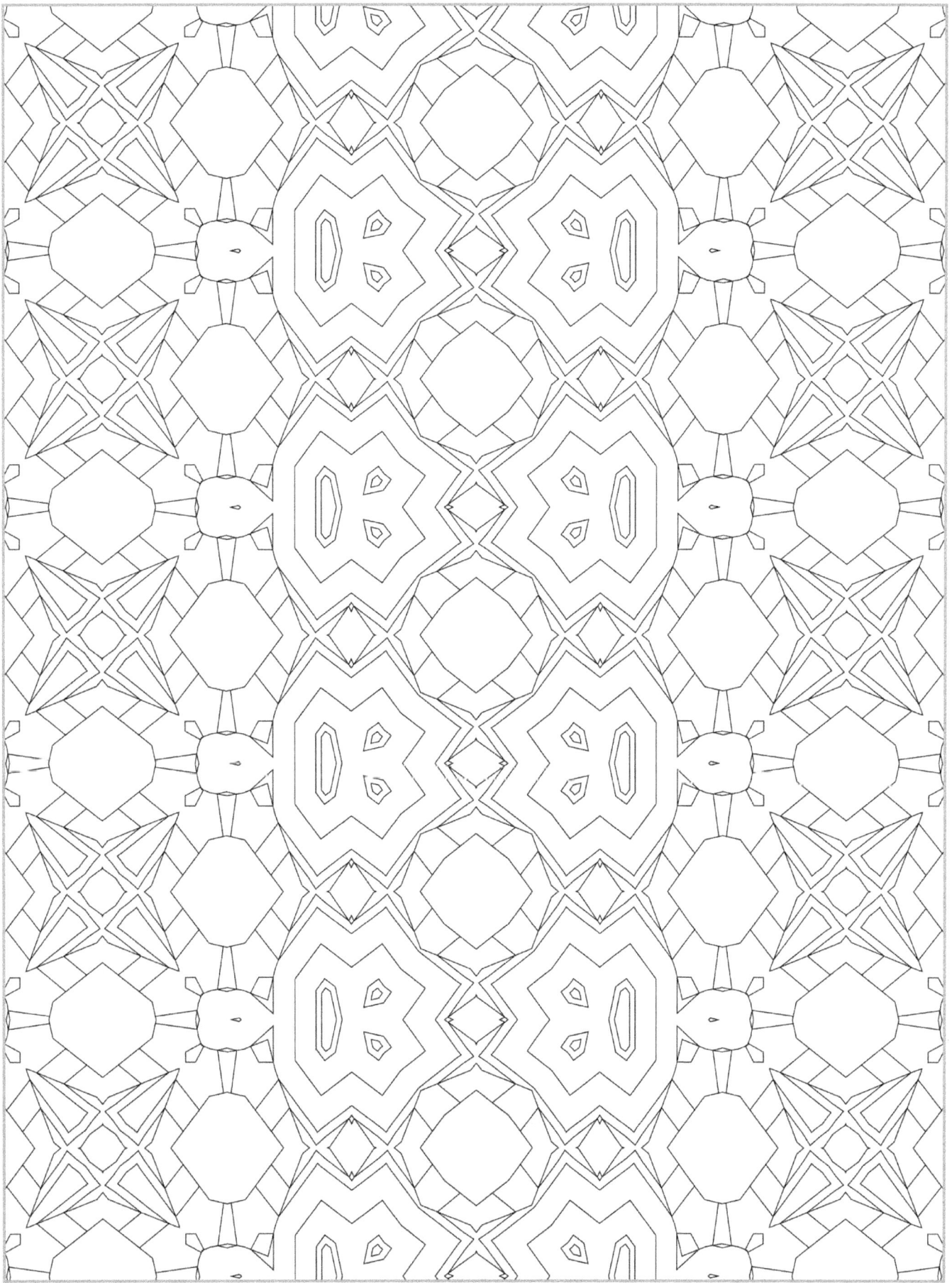

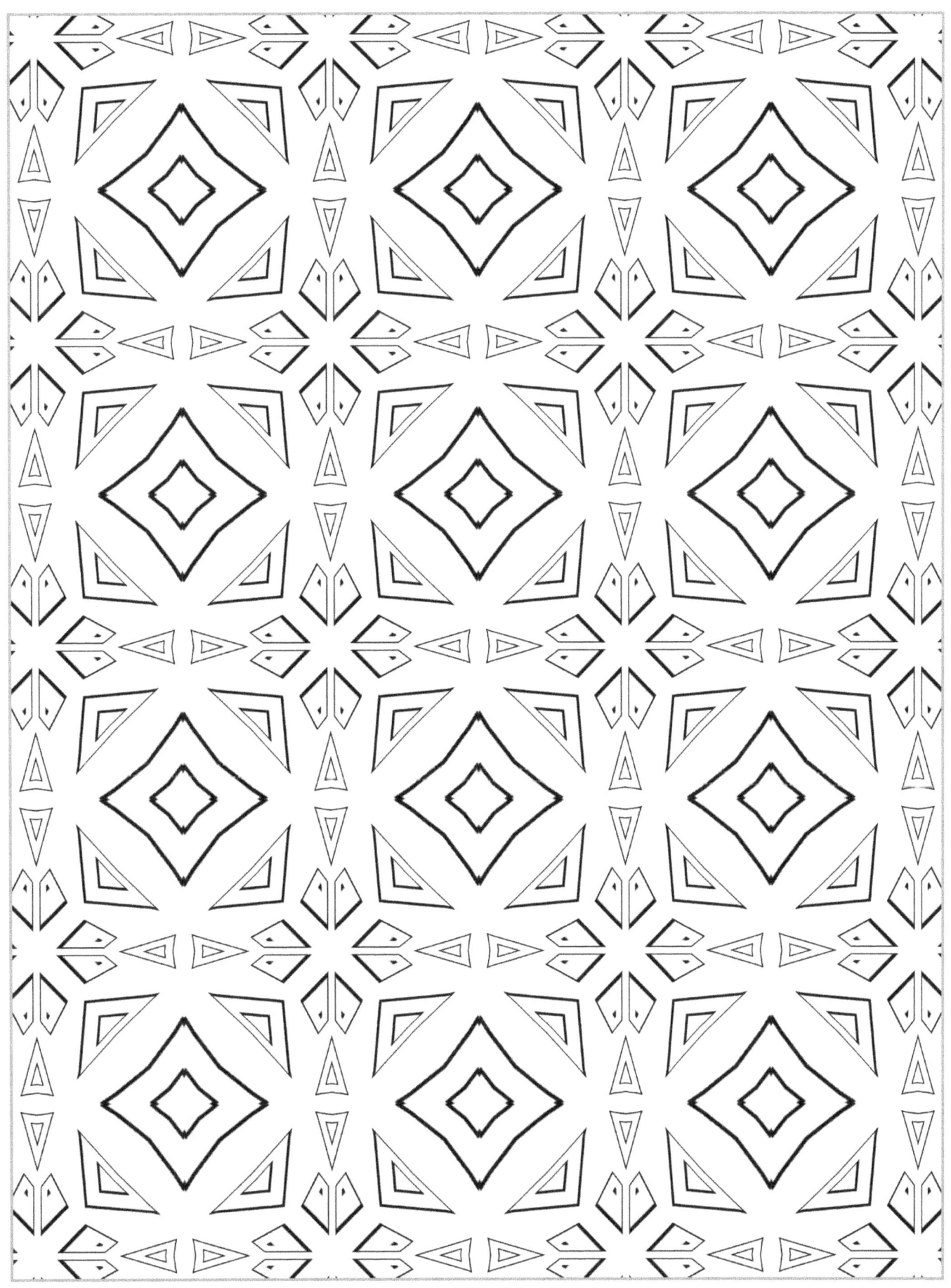

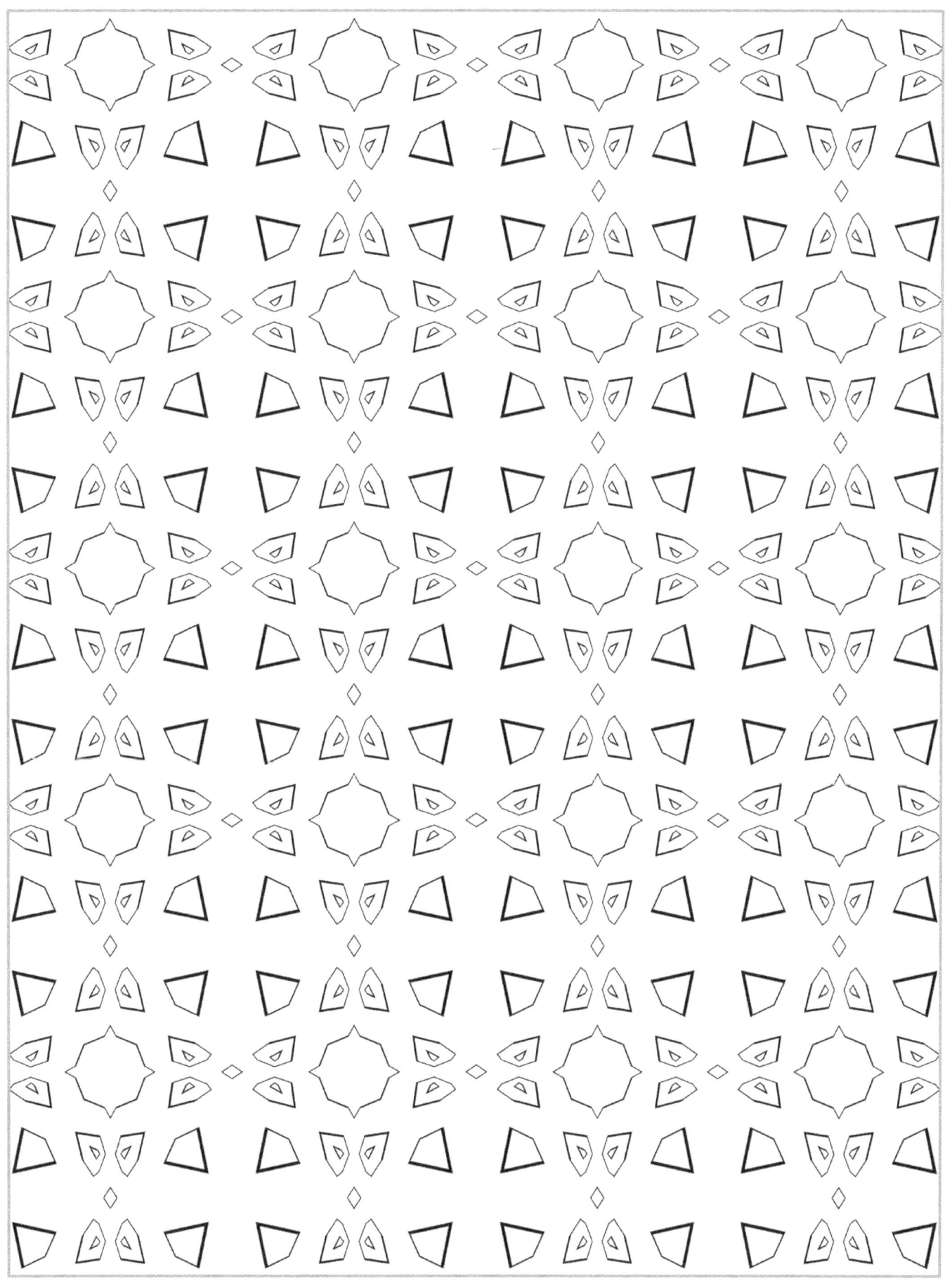

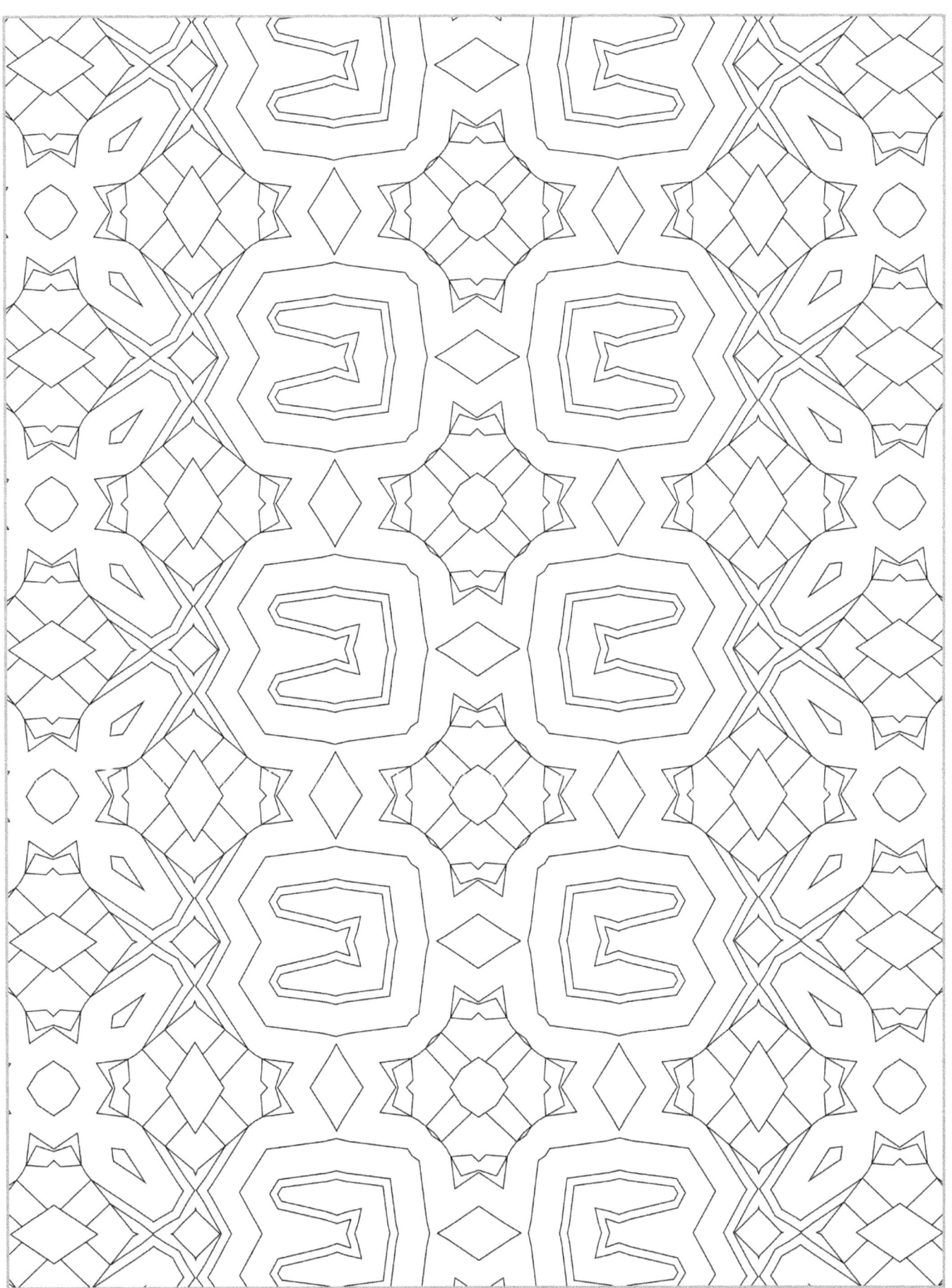

www.ingramcontent.com/pod-product-compliance
Lightning Source LLC
Chambersburg PA
CBHW080833180526
45168CB00006B/2663